I0518728

Officially Published LLC

www.officiallyhalee.com

To request permissions, contact the publisher at:
info@officiallypublished.com

ISBN: 9798990956872

Illustrations: Artificial Intelligence generated with
prompts written by Officially Halee.

THIS JOURNAL BELONGS TO:

_____

Wonder.

Always allow your imagination to wander and never lose your sense of whimsy in life.

Do not use this journal <u>just to</u> write homework assignments, book reports, and English papers.

USE THIS JOURNAL TO EXPRESS YOURSELF.

Write down your feelings...Or not write your feelings. Write a story....or not write a story.

Write whatever you want. Write whoever you are.

As a teenager, I think society places too many expectations for youth.

BE WHOEVER YOU ARE.
WRITE WHOEVER YOU ARE.

OFFICIALLY HALEE, TEEN AUTHOR

YOU HAVE WORDS WRITE THEM.

Express your thoughts, uncork your imagination to take you to new heights and enjoy expressing yourself.

This journal contains blank and lined pages. Your imagination knows no bounds and neither does this journal. Write whatever you want, doodle whatever you want.

Words are the center of our lives. Our thoughts, the music in our headphones, the scripts for our favorite TV shows and movies.

SO, WHY NOT TAKE PRIDE IN YOUR WRITING?

I am referring to more than homework, English papers, and what the world considers "writing". Writing is art, it cannot be bound by logic or others' expectations.

Writing is how you create it.

I CREATED THIS JOURNAL BECAUSE I WANT EVERYONE IN THE WORLD TO FEEL COMFORTABLE EXPRESSING THEMSELVES THROUGH WORDS.

I first began writing at seven years old. I started by writing personal narratives, then daily journal entries and eventually stories that became published books.

I WROTE BECAUSE I ENJOYED IT.

My parents made it a daily habit for me to write for at least fifteen minutes. I started by writing daily entries about my life. Then, it became more imaginative. I started writing in dialogue, creating characters and plot lines. I was just an eight-year -old girl, loving the daily habit of writing for fifteen minutes a day.

BY THE END OF THIRD GRADE, I WROTE AN ENTIRE BOOK.

Writing can take you anywhere, you just have to start.

REMOVE ALL OF THE VOICES IN YOUR HEAD, AND LISTEN TO YOUR OWN.

This journal is for your thoughts. Write whoever you are, this is a safe space for you.

OFFICIALLY HALEE, TEEN AUTHOR & PHILANTHROPIST

SCAN THE QR CODE TO WATCH
THE INTRODUCTION VIDEO.

This journal is all about who you are.

On the next page, write all the words you think describe who you are.

tip! Use a thesaurus to expand your vocabulary.

OFFICIALLY

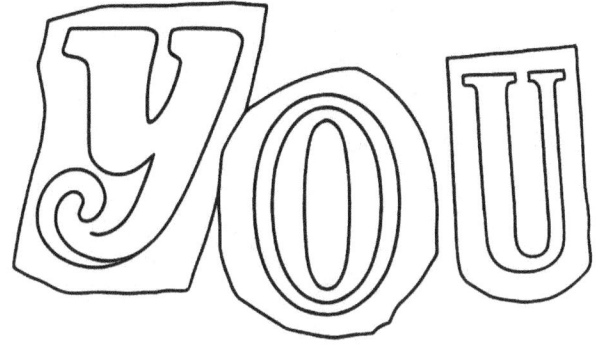

Write Life.

Write Plans.

Write Essays.

Write Thoughts

Write Stories.

Write Possibilities.

WRITE WHOEVER

YOU ARE.

WRITE NOW.

www.ingramcontent.com/pod-product-compliance
Lightning Source LLC
Chambersburg PA
CBHW070914130626

46555CB00001B/130